SAINSBURY'S

Quick and Easy
Beans and Pulses

Wendy Godfrey

D1079997

Contents

3   **Introduction**

6   **Soups and Starters**

20   **Fish**

34   **Meat**

46   **Salads and Vegetables**

56   **Vegetarian Dishes**

72   **Party Dishes**

80   **Index**

Published exclusively for J Sainsbury plc
Stamford House Stamford Street
London SE1 9LL
by Martin Books
Simon & Schuster Consumer Group
Grafton House 64 Maids Causeway
Cambridge CB5 8DD

Published 1996
ISBN 0 85941 938 X
© 1996 Martin Books
All rights reserved

Printed and bound in the UK by Bath Press Colourbooks
Design: Green Moore Lowenhoff
Photography: Steve Lee
Styling: Jo Harris
Food preparation: Wendy Lee
Typesetting: Cambridge Photosetting Services
Pictured on the front cover: Quick Cassoulet (page 78)

Introduction

Although baked beans have long been a British favourite, beans and pulses have truly come into their own with the rise in vegetarianism. They are also used to great effect in many fish and meat-based dishes, and are very healthy, being low in fat and high in fibre and starch. Another reason for the increasing popularity of beans and pulses is that they are inexpensive, and many are now conveniently packaged in cans for use in quick-and-easy recipes. The range in both the canned and dried varieties is enormous.

The term pulses includes the whole group of beans, as well as chick peas, lentils and split and dried peas. The recipes in this book use a great many of the canned and dried beans and pulses that are now widely available, including those which are ready-flavoured. On the whole, bean varieties can be interchanged, e.g. haricot beans can be substituted with flageolet beans, reduced-sugar-and-salt baked beans can replace ordinary baked beans – so do aim to try a few new types.

Beans and pulses are a staple ingredient in many parts of the world: they feature strongly in South American and Mexican foods like tacos and chilli con carne. Lentils and chick peas are found in many Indian and Middle Eastern dishes such as dahls, hummus and felafels. Most of these traditional dishes are inexpensive because herbs and spices are used as flavourings and little, if any, meat or fish is added. With the massive quantity of baked beans in tomato sauce consumed in Britain one might think that beans are native to this country. In fact, we import beans from America to make our baked beans, and the dish is actually a derivation of Boston baked beans.

THE NUTRITIONAL VALUE OF PULSES

Today's nutrition guidelines suggest that we should follow a diet containing plenty of starchy foods, and that we should reduce the amount of fat, salt and sugar we consume. There are few ingredients better than beans and pulses to use as a basis for main meal dishes. Not only are they an excellent source of protein and rich in starch and fibre, but they contain little fat and salt, especially if you choose beans canned in water rather than brine.

While most of us know that meat, fish, eggs and dairy products are good sources of protein, we sometimes forget that rice, pulses and cereals also provide protein. If you rely mainly on these for your protein, do be sure to combine them in your meals. The combination of pulses with rice or cereals is important in providing your body with the complete protein it needs. So, for example, rice and peas is a good protein source, as is lentils and pasta. This food combining doesn't require a lot of thought – it's as simple as beans on toast!

Beans and pulses are also a rich source of the range of B-vitamins (except B12, which is found only in foods of animal origin). B-vitamins are needed for the release of energy from food so that it can be used by the body. Beans also contain iron which forms part of red blood cells and helps to circulate oxygen. The other significant mineral in beans is phosphorus which helps to keep bones and teeth strong.

COOKING METHODS

Cooking beans from their dried state does not seem to fit in very well with the concept of 'quick and easy' dishes. It is much more convenient to use canned beans, which have been prepared for you. However, dried beans can be prepared and cooked in advance, and then frozen, ready for use in salads, soups or other dishes (see below). This will also cut the cost when preparing food for large numbers. As a rough guide, prepared beans will double in weight from dried. For example, a 250 g (8 oz) packet of black beans will produce 500 g (1 lb) of cooked beans. When cooking beans and pulses, follow the instructions given on the packet. Most packets will suggest conventional cooking methods as well as giving microwave instructions. A pressure cooker will also cut down on cooking time, but you must follow the instructions for your own equipment.

STORING COOKED BEANS

Cooked beans can be covered and stored in the refrigerator for 2–3 days, or frozen in freezer bags or airtight containers. Soak and cook according to the packet instructions. Rinse in cold water after cooking and drain in a colander or large sieve for at least 30 minutes. Decant into freezer bags or containers and seal well. Label and date. Frozen beans will keep in good condition for at least six months.

Warning: It is essential to follow the packet instructions when cooking beans with regard to the 10-minute boiling before simmering. There is a toxin present in some beans, particularly the red kidney variety, which can cause severe gastro-enteritis unless the beans are boiled for at least 10 minutes. Canned beans are quite safe as they have been through this boiling procedure as part of the canning process.

BEAN VARIETIES

Aduki Beans These are also known as Adzuki beans. They are small and shiny with an attractive red-brown colour and are imported from China and Thailand. Their flavour is earthy and slightly sweet. They are available dried or in cans.

Black Beans These are currently only available dried. Small and black, they are much used in the cooking of South America, Mexico and Spain. Ready-prepared fermented black beans are often used in Chinese dishes. Black bean sauce in jars can be found with the Chinese ingredients in the supermarket.

Black-eyed Beans As their name suggests, these beans have a small black marking on their creamy coloured skin. They come mainly from America and are also known as black-eyed peas or cow peas. They are available dried and canned, and are one of the ingredients in canned mixed pulses.

Borlotti Beans These attractive cream and pink speckled beans come from Italy, Spain and Africa. They are available dried or canned and are often included in canned mixed beans.

Butter Beans One of the best known beans in British cooking (although they come from Madagascar), these are large and flat with a creamy colour. They are inclined to go mushy if overcooked, and are available dried or canned.

Cannellini Beans These are from Italy and are much used in the cuisine of that country. They are a white variety of the red kidney bean and are available dried or canned.

Flageolet Beans These are a variety of the haricot bean and are harvested while still in the pod, which explains their attractive pale green colour. They are imported from France and used extensively in French recipes. They are available dried and canned.

Haricot Beans These are probably the most commonly consumed beans in the UK as they are used to make the ubiquitous baked beans in tomato sauce. They are available dried and canned.

Mung Beans These tiny olive green beans come from Thailand, China and Australia. They are best known in their sprouted form – as bean sprouts, but they are also available dried.

Pinto Beans These resemble borlotti beans with their attractive pink and brown speckles. They are used in both American and Mexican cooking. They are available dried and canned. Pinto beans are also used to make re-fried beans in Mexican cooking.

Red Kidney Beans With their distinctive dark red colour and firm mealy texture, these American beans are very versatile. They are available dried, canned and prepared in chilli sauce.

Soya Beans These are available in many guises and are naturally rich in protein. They are available canned, but are also ground into soya flour from which meat substitutes are made. Soya milk and bean curd are other by-products of the soya bean.

RECIPE NOTES

All the recipes in this book give ingredients in both metric (g, ml, etc.) and imperial (oz, pints, etc.) measures. Use either set of quantities, but not a mixture of both, in any one recipe.

All teaspoons and tablespoons are level, unless otherwise stated.
1 teaspoon = a 5 ml spoon:
1 tablespoon = a 15 ml spoon.

Egg size is medium, unless otherwise stated.

Vegetables and fruit are medium-sized unless otherwise stated.

Freshly ground black pepper should be used throughout.

OTHER TYPES OF PULSES

Lentils These come in red, yellow, pale green and the king of lentils, Puy, with its slatey, blue-green colour. The red and yellow lentils lose their shape and cook to a mush quite quickly, and are used in many Middle Eastern and Indian dishes. The green lentils are used more commonly in European dishes. They are available dried and canned.

Chick Peas These look like skinless golden hazelnuts. They are used in Indian and Mediterranean cooking, and are also known as garbanzo beans. They are available dried and canned.

Marrowfat Peas These are usually available whole in cans, but are also popularly known in England as mushy peas. The dried version is pale green in colour.

Split Peas These peas (either yellow or green) have had their skins removed and have been split in half. The yellow variety is the most common and is available dried or as pease pudding.

Gungo Peas These are available in cans and are used in West Indian cooking. They are yellow and brown dried peas which have been processed.

PREPARATION AND COOKING TIMES

Preparation and cooking times are included at the head of the recipes as a general guide: preparation times, especially, are approximate and timings are usually rounded to the nearest 5 minutes.

Preparation times include the time taken to prepare ingredients in the list, but not to make any 'basic' recipe.

The cooking times given at the heads of the recipes denote cooking periods when the dish can be left largely unattended, e.g. baking, and not the total amount of cooking time for the recipe. Always read and follow the timings given for the steps of the recipe in the method.

Soups and Starters

All the soups in this section are winter warmers. However, as in Britain we do get chilly days even in midsummer, don't feel too restricted by this seasonal aspect! Soups make good quick lunches when served with bread, salad and perhaps a pâté or spread – try the hummus-inspired Bean Dip on page 12. Felafels (page 16) would also be good served with soup as a light dinner or hearty lunch.

Black Bean and Orange Soup

Preparation time: 10 minutes + overnight soaking + 15 minutes cooking.
Freezing: recommended. Serves 4–6.

Canned red kidney beans can always be substituted for black beans and are more convenient than soaking black beans overnight. This recipe is from the southern USA, although variations can be found in Mexico and South America.

2 tablespoons sunflower oil
1 onion, chopped finely
1 red pepper, de-seeded and chopped finely
4 rashers streaky bacon, chopped
350 g (12 oz) cooked black beans
   (see page 4) or 420 g can of red kidney
   beans, rinsed and drained

1 orange, quartered with pips removed
1 tablespoon wine vinegar
750 ml (1¼ pints) stock or water
salt and freshly ground black pepper

❶ Heat the oil in a saucepan and gently fry the onion, pepper and bacon for 5 minutes.
❷ Add the beans, orange quarters, vinegar and stock or water.

❸ Bring to the boil, cover and simmer for 10 minutes, or until the beans are very soft.
❹ Remove the orange quarters, squeezing the juice into the soup.
❺ Season to taste and serve.

Pea Soup with Bacon

**Preparation time: 10 minutes + overnight soaking
+ 2 hours cooking.**
Freezing: recommended. Serves 6.

This is the traditional London pea soup after which the winter fogs
were nicknamed. It is unlikely that many people remember the times
before our cities became smokeless zones, but this soup can still be
enjoyed when the weather is cold and you're in need of comfort food.

50 g (2 oz) butter

1 onion, chopped finely

200 g (7 oz) bacon rashers or offcuts, chopped

2 celery sticks, sliced

375 g (12 oz) dried green peas, soaked
overnight and drained

1.75 litres (3 pints) ham stock

grated zest and juice of 1 lemon

1 tablespoon chopped fresh mint

salt and freshly ground black pepper

❶ Heat the butter in a large saucepan
and gently fry the onion and bacon for
about 5 minutes.

❷ Add the celery and fry for 5 minutes
more.

❸ Add the drained peas to the pan with
the stock and lemon zest and juice.

❹ Bring to the boil, and then lower the
heat and simmer for 1¼ hours.

❺ If you like a chunky soup, add the
mint, season to taste and serve. If you
prefer a smooth soup, whizz in a food
processor or liquidiser before adding the
mint and seasoning.

Bean Cappuccino Soup

Preparation time: 5 minutes + 15 minutes cooking.
Freezing: not recommended. Serves 4–6.

Several well-known chefs have laid claim to inventing this style of soup. With its frothy top, it resembles a cappuccino, and looks best when served in a large Continental-style coffee cup. A blender or liquidiser will create the most froth, although a food processor will work too.

1 onion, chopped

2 garlic cloves, sliced

1 tablespoon vegetable oil

2 × 420 g cans of butter beans, drained
and rinsed

900 ml (1½ pints) vegetable stock

200 g tub of crème fraîche

salt and freshly ground black pepper

fresh chopped parsley or crispy onions topping,
to garnish

❶ Gently fry the onion and garlic in the oil until softened but not browned.

❷ Add the beans and stock, and bring to the boil. Lower the heat and simmer for 10 minutes.

❸ Whizz in a blender, liquidiser or processor and return to the pan.

❹ Stir in the crème fraîche and adjust the seasoning. Bring to the boil and whizz once again, before pouring into warm serving cups. Sprinkle with the garnish and serve at once.

Tomato and Bean Soup

Preparation time: 5 minutes + 20 minutes cooking.
Freezing: recommended. Serves 4.

Canned beans and tomatoes make this a really speedy soup to prepare. You can use any white or pale beans. Serve this soup with fresh crusty bread.

1 tablespoon olive oil

1 onion, chopped finely

2 garlic cloves, crushed

420 g can of black-eyed beans, rinsed
and drained

400 g can of chopped tomatoes

1.2 litres (2 pints) vegetable stock

2 tablespoons tomato purée

2 tablespoons red pesto sauce

grated parmesan, to serve

salt and freshly ground black pepper

❶ Heat the oil in a large saucepan and fry the onion and garlic gently for 5 minutes.

❷ Add the beans, tomatoes, stock and purée.

❸ Bring to the boil, and then lower the heat and simmer for 10 minutes.

❹ Stir in the pesto with the seasoning to taste. Sprinkle with parmesan before serving.

Curried Lentil and Spinach Soup

Preparation time: 10 minutes + 30 minutes cooking.
Freezing: recommended. Serves 4–6.

This is a thinner version of a dahl, the traditional lentil accompaniment to curries. It is suitable for vegetarians and is good on a cold day as a starter before a pilau or biriani. Use whatever strength curry powder or paste you prefer.

2 tablespoons sunflower oil
1 onion, chopped finely
2 garlic cloves, crushed
2 tablespoons curry powder or paste

250 g (8 oz) packet of fresh spinach, rinsed
175 g (6 oz) red lentils
1 litre (1¾ pints) vegetable stock
salt and freshly ground black pepper

❶ Heat the oil in a saucepan and gently fry the onion and garlic for a few minutes.

❷ Stir in the curry powder or paste and the spinach. Cover and cook for 3 minutes, or until the spinach has collapsed.

❸ Add the lentils and stock, bring to the boil and then lower the heat and simmer for 15 minutes.

❹ Season to taste and either serve as it is, or blend until smooth in a liquidiser or food processor, reheat and serve.

Bean Dip and Crudités

Preparation time: 10 minutes.
Freezing: not recommended. Serves 6.

This is a version of hummus using flageolet beans instead of chick peas. I have suggested Mediterranean-style accompaniments as 'dippers'.

400 g can of flageolet beans, drained
    and rinsed
4 tablespoons tahini paste
grated zest and juice of 2 lemons
grated zest and juice of 1 lime
2 tablespoons natural yogurt
1 teaspoon garlic purée
salt and freshly ground black pepper

a sprinkling of paprika or 2 sliced salad
    onions, to garnish
For the dippers:
toasted french stick slices; hard-boiled eggs;
    quartered tomatoes; courgette sticks; carrot
    sticks; fennel quarters; raw mushrooms;
    pepper strips; lightly cooked french beans;
    celery sticks

❶ Blend together the first six ingredients in a blender or food processor. Season to taste.

❷ Transfer to a serving bowl and garnish.

❸ Prepare the dippers, according to season or what you have on hand, and arrange on a serving plate.

Filo Parcels

Preparation time: 10 minutes + 15 minutes baking.
Freezing: recommended. Makes 18.

Although a cinch to make, these pastry bundles always look so
spectacular that nobody will believe you made them yourself! They
could be served with peperonata, which is simply sliced and de-seeded
peppers cooked slowly with garlic in olive oil.

400 g packet of frozen filo pastry, defrosted
447 g can of mixed beans in a spicy pepper
  sauce

1 red pepper, de-seeded and chopped
50 g (2 oz) butter, melted
salt and freshly ground black pepper

❶ Preheat the oven to Gas Mark 5/190°C/
375°F.
❷ Cut the pastry into 15 cm (6-inch)
squares, keeping the filo covered when
not in use.
❸ Layer four squares to form a sixteen-
point star.
❹ Mix the beans with the chopped
pepper, and season to taste.
❺ Put one tablespoon of filling in the
centre of the filo star and gather together
to create a parcel. Place on a lightly
greased baking tray.
❻ Repeat with the remaining filo pastry
and filling, leaving plenty of space
between each parcel on the baking tray
(use two trays, if necessary).
❼ Brush the parcels with melted butter
and bake for 10–15 minutes, until crisp
and golden.

Felafels

Preparation time: 10 minutes + 10 minutes cooking.
Freezing: recommended. Serves 4.

Canned chick peas certainly save time when you are making these spicy
Middle Eastern vegetarian patties. They are usually quite small and
therefore ideal as a starter, but these ones are a bit larger and ideal to
serve with a salad for a quick lunch or snack.

420 g canned chick peas, rinsed, drained,
   and chopped finely
1 onion, grated
1 garlic clove, crushed
1 teaspoon each ground coriander and cumin
¼ teaspoon cayenne pepper
1 tablespoon chopped fresh coriander
2 tablespoons wholewheat flour, seasoned

2 tablespoons vegetable oil
salt and freshly ground black pepper
To serve:
4 tablespoons natural Greek-style yogurt
1 tablespoon chopped fresh coriander
1 lemon, quartered
4 sprigs of coriander

❶ Mix together the chick peas, onion
and garlic.
❷ Stir in the spices and chopped
coriander, and season to taste.
❸ Shape the mixture into four small
patties.
❹ Coat them in seasoned wholemeal
flour.
❺ Heat the oil in a frying-pan and cook
the patties for 4 minutes on each side, or
until golden brown.
❻ Meanwhile, blend the yogurt and
chopped coriander together and season
to taste.
❼ Serve the felafels on individual plates
with a tablespoon of the yogurt. Garnish
each with a lemon quarter and coriander
sprig.

Borlotti Bruschetta

Preparation time: 10 minutes + 10 minutes cooking.
Freezing: not recommended.
Serves 6 as a starter or 4 as a snack.

Bruschetta are usually made with toasted ciabatta bread, but you could use toasted baguette slices instead. Choose your favourite antipasti range as toppers.

285 g jar of mixed pepper antipasti or
    other antipasti
420 g can of borlotti beans, rinsed and drained

4–6 garlic cloves
1 ciabatta loaf, cut in 1.5 cm (½-inch) slices
4 sprigs of basil, sliced thinly

❶ Drain the oil from the antipasti and put 2 tablespoons in a frying-pan. Reserve the rest.

❷ Add the beans to the pan with two crushed garlic cloves. Heat for 2 minutes, stirring occasionally.

❸ Toast the bread on both sides. Cut the remaining garlic cloves in half and rub the cut sides into the toast. Drizzle with the reserved oil.

❹ Spoon the beans over the toast and arrange the antipasti on top.

❺ Garnish with basil and serve at once.

Prosciutto Rolls

Preparation time: 10 minutes.
Freezing: not recommended. Serves 4.

Gammon and pease pudding are traditionally served together, so I created a starter combining these two complementary flavours.

220 g can of pease pudding
2 tablespoons mayonnaise
1 tablespoon chopped fresh chives
70 g packet of prosciutto

freshly ground black pepper
To garnish:
4 pickled cucumbers or 12 gherkins
a few salad leaves

❶ Blend together the pease pudding, mayonnaise and chives using a fork or electric whisk. Season with freshly ground black pepper.

❷ Divide the prosciutto into 8 pieces, and then spread each piece with the pease pudding mixture.

❸ Roll the prosciutto up and refrigerate until ready to serve.

❹ Arrange the cucumbers or gherkins and salad leaves on four plates with the prosciutto rolls.

Fish

The choice of beans and pulses to go with fish dishes needs careful consideration so that they do not overwhelm the delicate flavours of fish.

The one exception to judicious flavouring is the recipe for Mexican Fishcakes (page 28). The robust South American cuisine adapts well to smoked fish, and the refried beans are a staple ingredient of Mexico.

Plaice Rolls with Watercress Sauce

Preparation time: 10 minutes + 20 minutes cooking.
Freezing: not recommended. Serves 4.

Any flat fish fillets could be used in this dish – lemon sole or dabs are equally good. Serve with a savoury rice.

4 plaice fillets

420 g can of green lentils, drained

250 g jar of Hollandaise sauce

12 sun-dried tomatoes

grated zest and juice of 1 lemon

75 g packet of watercress

salt and freshly ground black pepper

❶ Preheat the oven to Gas Mark 5/180°C/ 350°F.

❷ Season the fillets with salt and pepper.

❸ Mix the lentils with two tablespoons of Hollandaise sauce and spread over the fillets.

❹ Arrange three sun-dried tomatoes across the middle of each fillet.

❺ Sprinkle with the lemon zest and juice.

❻ Roll the fillets up and fasten with toothpicks. Arrange them in a baking dish and brush with a little oil from the sun-dried tomatoes. Bake for 20 minutes.

❼ Meanwhile, to make the sauce, whizz the remaining Hollandaise sauce with the watercress. Season and serve with the cooked fish.

Green Fish Pie

Preparation time: 15 minutes + 20 minutes cooking.
Freezing: not recommended. Serves 4–6.

Potato topped pies are popular and help to 'stretch' whatever ingredients are to be found underneath. Marrowfat or processed peas are almost as inexpensive as potatoes, and they purée beautifully.

500 g (1 lb) white fish fillets (e.g. cod, haddock or hoki)
300 ml (½ pint) milk
1 packet of béchamel sauce mix
3 tablespoons chopped fresh parsley
250 g (8 oz) courgettes, sliced

1 tablespoon chopped fresh mint
540 g can of marrowfat, processed or garden peas
50 g (2 oz) butter
2 tablespoons single cream
salt and freshly ground black pepper

❶ Cook the fish on a plate with two tablespoons of milk in the microwave (for a 650W/B oven cook for 5 minutes on HIGH; for a 750W/D oven cook for 4 minutes on HIGH).

❷ Meanwhile, make up the béchamel sauce using the rest of the milk. Drain the fish liquor into the sauce.

❸ Skin and flake the fish and mix gently with the sauce and chopped parsley.

❹ Season and put in the bottom of a heatproof dish.

❺ Arrange the courgettes over the top and sprinkle with the chopped mint. Season again.

❻ Heat the peas in a saucepan until just below boiling point. Preheat the grill.

❼ Drain and purée them in a blender or food processor with the butter and cream.

❽ Spread the purée over the pie and rough up with a fork.

❾ Grill until golden and hot through.

Silver Moon Salmon Steaks

Preparation time: 10 minutes + 15 minutes cooking.
Freezing: recommended before cooking if using fresh salmon.
Serves 4.

You can serve these salmon steaks in their foil 'moon' parcels to open at the table. The flavour is oriental in style, and would go well with fried rice.

160 g bottle of black bean sauce
2 garlic cloves, chopped finely
2.5 cm (1-inch) piece of fresh root ginger, chopped finely
2 tablespoons dry sherry

oil, for brushing
4 × 175 g (6 oz) salmon steaks, rinsed and patted dry
12 seedless green grapes, halved
4 chopped salad onions, to garnish

❶ Heat the oven to Gas Mark 5/190°C/375°F.

❷ Mix together the black bean sauce, garlic, ginger and sherry.

❸ Oil four large squares of kitchen foil and place a salmon steak towards one end of each.

❹ Divide the black bean sauce into four portions and spread on top of the steaks.

Arrange six grape halves on top of each steak.

❺ Fold the foil over the top of the salmon and crimp the edges to seal the parcels into semi-circular 'moon' shapes.

❻ Put the parcels on a baking sheet and bake for 15 minutes. Serve the parcels unopened with a bowl of chopped salad onions to garnish.

Smoked Haddock Tortillas

Preparation time: 10 minutes + 20 minutes cooking.
Freezing: recommended before step 6.
Serves 4 as a main course or 8 as a starter.

Serve this Mexican-inspired dish with a ready-made chilli or taco sauce and some soured cream or Greek-style yogurt.

500 g (1 lb) smoked haddock fillets
336 g packet of 8 tortillas
453 g can of refried beans
2 each green and red peppers, de-seeded
   and chopped

400 g can of chopped tomatoes
Tabasco sauce, to taste
1 packet of coriander leaves,
   chopped roughly
salt and freshly ground black pepper

❶ Poach the haddock in water, or microwave it. (For a 650W/B oven cook for 5 minutes on HIGH; for a 750W/D oven cook for 4 minutes on HIGH.) Drain and flake. Preheat the grill.
❷ Spread the tortillas within an inch of the edges with the refried beans.

❸ Mix the flaked fish with the peppers and tomatoes, and spoon over the top.
❹ Sprinkle each with a drop of Tabasco sauce and the chopped coriander.
❺ Season well and fold into parcels.
❻ Grill for about 5 minutes on either side and serve hot.

Prawns with Broad Beans and Potatoes

Preparation time: 10 minutes + 20 minutes cooking.
Freezing: not recommended. Serves 4.

This summer dish is easy to prepare in advance. Add the prawns at the very last minute to keep them as fresh as possible.

500 g (1 lb) new potatoes, scrubbed
3 sprigs of fresh mint
500 g (1 lb) broad beans, fresh or frozen
150 g tub of natural yogurt
150 ml (¼ pint) mayonnaise

250 g (8 oz) peeled prawns, defrosted
   if frozen
1 tablespoon chopped fresh parsley
salt and freshly ground black pepper
lemon wedges, to garnish

❶ Boil the potatoes in their skins with the mint for 20 minutes. Drain and cool.
❷ Cook the beans for 10 minutes in lightly salted boiling water, and then rinse in cold water and pop off the skins.
❸ Slice the cooled potatoes and mix with the beans.

❹ Mix together the yogurt and mayonnaise and fold in the potatoes and beans. Transfer to a serving dish and season to taste. Cover and refrigerate until ready to serve.
❺ Before serving, stir in the prawns and parsley and garnish with lemon wedges.

Mexican Fishcakes

Preparation time: 15 minutes + 30 minutes cooking.
Freezing: recommended. Serves 4.

The rough texture of refried beans blends well with mashed potato and fish, while chilli sauce adds that authentic dash of Mexican flavour. Serve with a tomato salsa or some guacamole.

250 g (8 oz) haddock fillet

25 g (1 oz) butter

2 tablespoons milk

500 g (1 lb) potatoes, peeled and chopped evenly

1–2 tablespoons chilli sauce

225 g can of refried beans

1 tablespoon chopped fresh coriander

1 egg, beaten

3 tablespoons maize meal or polenta

salt and freshly ground black pepper

oil, for frying

❶ Lay the fish on a heatproof plate with the butter and milk. Season well.

❷ Put the potatoes in a pan of lightly salted boiling water and place the plate of fish on top. Cover the fish with the saucepan's lid so that the fish steams in the heat of the boiling potatoes.

❸ Cook for 20–25 minutes, or until both potatoes and fish are cooked. Drain the potatoes and mash with the buttery juices from the fish. Beat in 1 tablespoon of chilli sauce.

❹ Remove the skin from the fish and discard. Flake the flesh and fold into the mashed potato along with the refried beans.

❺ Add the coriander and then loosen the mixture, if necessary, with either another tablespoon of chilli sauce or milk.

❻ Shape into eight round patties.

❼ Dip the patties into the beaten egg, and then coat with maize meal or polenta.

❽ Heat 2.5 cm (½-inch) of oil in a frying-pan and cook the fishcakes for 3–5 minutes on each side, until crisp and golden.

❾ Drain on kitchen paper.

Tuna and Beans au Gratin

Preparation time: 10 minutes + 15 minutes cooking.
Freezing: recommended. Serves 2.

Choose a well flavoured cheese for this dish. The beans make a speedy alternative to pasta. Serve with a crisp green salad.

300 ml (½ pint) milk
25 g (1 oz) butter
25 g (1 oz) plain flour
1 tablespoon chopped capers
1 tablespoon chopped fresh parsley
425 g can of cannellini beans, drained

75 g (3 oz) cheese, grated
200 g can of tuna in brine, drained
   and flaked
2 tomatoes, sliced thinly
2 tablespoons dried breadcrumbs
salt and freshly ground black pepper

❶ Put the milk, butter and flour in a pan and heat slowly, whisking constantly. Bring to the boil and cook for 1 minute.
❷ Stir in the capers, parsley, beans and two-thirds of the cheese.
❸ Fold the tuna into the mixture and heat through gently. Preheat the grill.
❹ Transfer the bean and tuna mixture to an ovenproof serving dish.
❺ Arrange the tomato slices around the edge of the dish.
❻ Mix the remaining cheese with the breadcrumbs and scatter in the centre.
❼ Grill until the top is golden brown, and serve immediately.

Herring and Bean Potato Nests

Preparation time: 10 minutes + 20 minutes cooking.
Freezing: recommended for potato nests only. Serves 4.

Instant mashed potato is very useful for piping.

186 g packet of instant mashed potato
1 tablespoon Dijon mustard
25 g (1 oz) butter
1 tablespoon cream or crème fraîche
220 g can of mixed bean salad

340 g jar of pickled or roll mop herrings,
   drained and cut in 2.5 cm (½-inch) strips
1 tablespoon chopped fresh dill or parsley
salt and freshly ground black pepper

❶ Preheat the oven to Gas Mark 6/200°C/400°F.
❷ Make up the potato according to the packet instructions and beat in the mustard, butter and cream or crème fraîche.
❸ Pipe the potato into four nests on an oiled baking tray, or use a spoon to shape the nests.
❹ Bake for 15–20 minutes, until golden brown, and then transfer to a warm serving plate.
❺ Meanwhile, mix together the bean salad, herring strips and herbs in a saucepan. Season to taste and heat gently.
❻ Drain away any excess liquid and then spoon the bean mixture into the cooked potato nests.

Grilled Trout with Puy Lentils

Preparation time: 10 minutes + 30 minutes cooking.
Freezing: recommended for the lentils only. Serves 4.

There are lentils and then there are lentils. These small slate-coloured lentils are the cream of the lentil crop.

They are called 'puy' lentils in reference to the peaks of the volcanic mountains in south-eastern France. With their lovely crunchy texture and dark shiny colour, these lentils make a stunning accompaniment to pink rainbow trout fillets. Serve with a radicchio salad.

1 tablespoon olive oil + extra for brushing

1 onion, chopped

2 garlic cloves, sliced

150 g packet of Puy lentils

125 g (4 fl oz) fish stock

125 g (4 fl oz) white wine

1 tablespoon chopped fresh parsley

4 rainbow trout fillets

1 lemon, halved

salt and freshly ground black pepper

❶ Heat the tablespoon of oil in a pan and fry the onion and garlic until soft but not browned.

❷ Add the lentils and toss to coat in oil.

❸ Pour in the stock and wine and bring to the boil.

❹ Cover and reduce to a simmer for 30 minutes, or until the liquid has been absorbed. Preheat the grill.

❺ Add the chopped parsley and seasoning to taste.

❻ While the lentils are cooking, brush the trout fillets with the remaining oil and the juice of half the lemon. Season.

❼ Grill for 3–4 minutes on each side, skin-side first, so that the fillets are ready at the same time as the lentils.

❽ Serve the lentils and trout on a platter, garnished with the other lemon half, cut in four wedges.

Meat

Many of the recipes in this section come under the peasant or comfort food category. What could be more satisfying than Yorkshire puddings with a tasty bean filling? For a lighter, more summery choice, try the Warm Duck and Bean Salad (page 44) or the Singapore Beef (page 42). The Chilli Ribs (see below) would taste delicious cooked over a barbecue.

Chilli Ribs

Preparation time: 5 minutes + 10 minutes cooking.
Freezing: recommended. Serves 2.

Pork ribs make an inexpensive meal and can now be bought ready-marinated, which cuts down considerably on the preparation time. Make sure you have plenty of paper napkins or tissues available for wiping sticky fingers.

375 g (12 oz) chilli-flavoured pork ribs
447 g can of chilli beans
1 onion, sliced thinly into rings

230 g can of chopped tomatoes
1 orange, scrubbed
salt and freshly ground black pepper

❶ Grill the ribs according to the packet instructions, turning frequently.

❷ Meanwhile, empty the beans into a pan and heat slowly with the onion rings and chopped tomatoes.

❸ Chop the whole orange, rind and flesh, and add to the pan. Heat through and season to taste.

❹ Serve the ribs on top of the beans.

Cowboy Barbecue Mince and Beans

Preparation time: 10 minutes + 20 minutes cooking.
Freezing: recommended. Serves 4.

Children love baked beans, and the family cook is always looking for new ways to serve them. There are some very good ready-prepared barbecue sauces available which add a delicious flavour to beans. This dish might also be used for a children's theme birthday party. Sausages or corned beef could be used instead of the minced beef.

1 tablespoon vegetable oil

1 onion, chopped

500 g (1 lb) minced beef

6 tablespoons barbecue sauce

2 tablespoons tomato purée

420 g can of baked beans

salt and freshly ground black pepper

❶ Heat the oil in a pan or flameproof casserole and fry the onion gently for 5 minutes.

❷ Add the minced beef and brown, stirring to break up the lumps.

❸ Stir in the barbecue sauce and tomato purée until well blended.

❹ Stir in the beans and cook until piping hot. Season to taste. The dish will keep well on a low heat for 30 minutes or so.

Lamb and Flageolets

Preparation time: 15 minutes + 15 minutes cooking.
Freezing: not recommended. Serves 4.

Beans and lamb are often served together in French country cooking. Although they are combined in this recipe, it would be possible to serve the beans on their own as a vegetarian dish.

1 tablespoon oil

1 red onion, sliced thinly

2 garlic cloves, sliced thinly

2 × 400 g cans of flageolet beans, rinsed and drained

6 sprigs of fresh rosemary

250 g carton of crème fraîche

4 thick chump lamb chops

salt and freshly ground black pepper

❶ Heat the oil in a pan and gently fry the onion and garlic until soft but not browned.

❷ Add the beans and two of the rosemary sprigs, chopped finely.

❸ Stir in the crème fraîche and heat to boiling. Transfer to a shallow serving dish and keep warm. Preheat the grill.

❹ Chop two more of the rosemary sprigs and press them into the lamb chops.

❺ Grill the chops for 5 minutes on either side, or until cooked to your liking. Season to taste and arrange the grilled chops on top of the beans.

❻ Garnish with the two remaining rosemary sprigs.

Pork and Cider Casserole

Preparation time: 10 minutes + 1½ hours cooking.
Freezing: recommended. Serves 4.

This rib-sticking casserole will warm you right through. Serve it with a leafy green vegetable. It takes only minutes to prepare, and can then be left to simmer without attention.

1 tablespoon vegetable oil

500 g (1 lb) diced casserole pork

1 onion, chopped

2 carrots, peeled and sliced

1 cooking apple, peeled, cored and sliced

150 g (6 oz) yellow split peas

1 tablespoon chopped fresh sage

4 bay leaves

300 ml (½ pint) cider

300 ml (½ pint) water

salt and freshly ground black pepper

❶ Heat the oil in a flameproof casserole and brown the pork, turning frequently.

❷ Scatter the onion, carrots and apple on the top. Cover with a tight-fitting lid and cook over a low heat for 10 minutes.

❸ Remove the lid and stir in the peas, herbs, cider and water. Bring to the boil and then lower the heat, cover and simmer for 1½ hours.

❹ Adjust the seasoning and serve.

Double Kidney with Dijon Mustard

Preparation time: 10 minutes + 15 minutes cooking.
Freezing: recommended. Serves 4.

Kidney beans are so called because of their shape. Here they are combined with lamb's kidneys in a quick but warming dish flavoured with Dijon mustard. It is good accompanied by a green leafy vegetable – cabbage, spinach or kale.

1 tablespoon vegetable oil

1 onion, chopped

6 lamb's kidneys, halved and cored

1 tablespoon flour, seasoned

300 ml (½ pint) lamb or chicken stock

1 tablespoon Dijon mustard

420 g can of red kidney beans, rinsed
  and drained

2 tablespoons chopped fresh parsley

salt and freshly ground black pepper

❶ Heat the oil in a pan or a flameproof casserole, and fry the onion until golden brown.

❷ Toss the kidney halves in seasoned flour and add to the pan. Stir and turn until cooked on all sides.

❸ Add the stock and mustard and bring to the boil. Reduce to a simmer and add the beans. Season to taste and bring back to the boil.

❹ Stir in 1 tablespoon of chopped parsley and sprinkle the rest on top. Serve at once.

Singapore Beef

**Preparation time: 10 minutes + 1 hour marinating
+ 15 minutes cooking.
Freezing: recommended. Serves 4.**

This spicy stir-fry dish uses a ready-made satay sauce to give it an authentic Singapore flavour.

500 g (1 lb) rump steak, cut in thin strips

190 g jar of satay sauce

1 onion, sliced

2 garlic cloves, chopped finely

2.5 cm (1-inch) piece of fresh root ginger,
    chopped finely

2 tablespoons vegetable oil

160 g jar of black bean sauce

3 tablespoons dark soy sauce

2 tablespoons red or white wine vinegar

6 salad onions, sliced

freshly ground black pepper

❶ Stir the beef strips into the satay sauce in a dish. Cover and refrigerate for at least one hour.

❷ Fry the onion, garlic and ginger in the oil until just beginning to brown.

❸ Add the marinated beef and satay sauce and stir-fry briskly until brown.

❹ Stir in the black bean sauce, soy sauce and vinegar, and simmer for 10 minutes.

❺ Season to taste. (It is quite likely that no salt will be needed.)

❻ Transfer to a serving dish and garnish with the sliced salad onions.

Warm Duck and Bean Salad

Preparation time: 10 minutes + 10 minutes cooking.
Freezing: not recommended. Serves 4.

This salad is ideal for a summer lunch or supper dish. The duck breasts can be cooked at the last minute and added to the salad bowl, which can be prepared ahead.

125 g (4 oz) french beans, trimmed
75 g packet of watercress, rinsed and dried
1 orange, sliced into 5 mm (¼-inch) rings
420 g can of pinto beans, drained and rinsed

50 g (2 oz) pitted black olives (optional)
2 duck breast fillets
2 tablespoons vinaigrette dressing

❶ Cook the french beans in lightly salted boiling water. Alternatively, microwave for 5 minutes on HIGH for a 650W/B oven, or for 4 minutes on HIGH for a 750W/D oven. Drain and rinse in cold water so that they keep their colour.

❷ Put the watercress, orange and pinto beans in a salad bowl with the olives, if using. Add the cooled french beans.

❸ Just before serving, grill the duck breasts for 4 minutes on either side. Slice thinly and add to the salad.

❹ Pour over the vinaigrette dressing along with any of the cooking juices (but not the fat) from the duck, and toss together. Serve immediately.

Sweet and Sour Chicken Yorkshires

Preparation time: 5 minutes + 20 minutes cooking.
Freezing: not recommended. Serves 4.

Ready-made Yorkshire puddings can be found in both the chilled and frozen food cabinets, in individual puddings or family size. They make an unusual container for savoury fillings – and you don't have to stick to roast beef.

12 individual Yorkshire puddings or 1 large
**   Yorkshire pudding**
2 boneless chicken breasts, seasoned
227 g can of bamboo shoots, drained

447 g can of mixed beans in sweet
**   and sour sauce**
6 salad onions, sliced
salt and freshly ground black pepper

❶ If you are cooking the Yorkshire puddings from raw, cook the seasoned chicken breasts in the same oven.

❷ If the puddings are ready-cooked, grill the chicken breasts for 5 minutes on each side, warming the puddings through in a low oven.

❸ Cut the cooked chicken into 2.5 cm (½-inch) cubes. Transfer to a small pan.

❹ Slice the bamboo shoots and add to the chicken with the mixed beans. Heat through and season to taste.

❺ Spoon the filling into the warmed puddings and garnish with the salad onions.

Salads and Vegetables

There are so many ways these days to cut down on preparation and cooking times without sacrificing on flavour. Canned beans in small quantities are ideal for adding extra starch and flavour to salads. Curry sauces, ready-made blinis and cans of flavoured beans are used to great effect in the recipes in this chapter.

Puy Lentil and Scallop Salad

Preparation time: 10 minutes + 20 minutes cooking.
Freezing: not recommended. Serves 4–6.

These small lentils from France have a nutty texture and are almost black when cooked, making an excellent foil for brightly coloured salad ingredients and fresh herbs. The small queen scallops cook very quickly, and their flavour goes well with bacon or other cured meats.

250 g packet of puy lentils
2 tablespoons olive oil
200 g (7 oz) queen scallops
125 g (4 oz) bacon cubes or pancetta, chopped

12 cherry tomatoes, halved
2 courgettes, sliced
1 red onion, chopped
2 tablespoons vinaigrette dressing
1 bunch of watercress, to serve

❶ Cook the lentils according to the packet instructions, then rinse and drain.
❷ Heat the oil in a pan and fry the scallops and bacon or pancetta.
❸ Toss together the prepared vegetables and drained lentils with the vinaigrette dressing.

❹ Add the hot scallops and bacon with the frying oil and toss again.
❺ Arrange the watercress around the edge of a serving platter and spoon the salad into the middle.

Bean Blinis

Preparation time: 10 minutes + 5 minutes cooking.
Freezing: not recommended. Serves 4.

These buckwheat pancakes can be bought ready-made, and make a quick base for all types of savoury toppings. They are traditionally served with smoked salmon or caviar, so I have kept to the fish theme here. Use any small can of beans in place of the butter beans.

200 g packet of four blinis
220 g can of butter beans, rinsed and drained
150 g tub of soured cream
250 g jar of marinated herring fillets, drained

1 dessert apple, cored and sliced and
  tossed in 2 teaspoons lemon juice
1 teaspoon chopped fresh chives

❶ Grill or toast the blinis on both sides until golden brown.
❷ Blend the beans with half the tub of soured cream and divide between the blinis.

❸ Top each blini with a herring fillet and a few apple slices.
❹ Garnish each with a dollop of soured cream and a sprinkling of chives.

Bean and Mushroom Tortilla

Preparation time: 10 minutes + 10 minutes cooking.
Freezing: not recommended.
Serves 2–6, depending on mealtime and hunger.

This is similar in style to a Spanish omelette – thick and chunky – and should be served cut in wedges. I used mixed beans in a curry sauce, but any canned beans in sauce could be substituted.

25 g (1 oz) butter
1 red onion, chopped finely
125 g (4 oz) mushrooms, sliced
447 g can of mixed beans in curry sauce

6 eggs, beaten
2 tablespoons chopped fresh coriander
salt and freshly ground black pepper

❶ Melt the butter in a non-stick or well-seasoned frying-pan and add the onion. Fry gently for 1 minute.
❷ Add the mushrooms and fry for 1 more minute.
❸ Mix the beans into the beaten eggs. Add the coriander and seasoning to taste. Preheat the grill to medium.

❹ Pour into the pan and cook for 5–6 minutes, until the bottom is set and golden. Put the pan under the grill for 4 minutes to set and brown the top.
❺ Slide the tortilla out on to a warm serving plate, and cut in wedges.

Broad Bean and Salami Salad

Preparation time: 10 minutes + 10 minutes cooking.
Freezing: not recommended. Serves 4.

The reason why some people do not like broad beans is because of the slight bitter taste of their skins. It is preferable to skin the beans for this salad, which is not as arduous a task as it may sound, as the beans are easily popped out from their skins once they are cooked. Choose your favourite salami from a packet or from the delicatessen counter. Serve with ciabatta bread to keep to the Italian theme.

500 g packet of frozen broad beans, cooked
   according to packet instructions
150 g (4 oz) thinly sliced salami, cut in bite-
   sized pieces
6 sun-dried tomatoes, sliced
1 tablespoon chopped fresh parsley

2 tablespoons olive oil or oil drained from the
   sun-dried tomatoes
1 teaspoon balsamic or wine vinegar
1 garlic clove, crushed
salt and freshly ground black pepper

❶ After cooking the beans, rinse them in cold water and pop the beans out of their skins. Discard the skins.

❷ Mix with the salami and sun-dried tomatoes in a serving bowl.

❸ Mix together the chopped parsley, oil, vinegar, garlic and seasoning.

❹ Pour over the salad and toss together well.

Mung Bean Dahl

Preparation time: 10 minutes + 30 minutes cooking.
Freezing: recommended (without the garnish). Serves 4.

Most dahls are made with lentils, but mung beans do not take much longer to cook and they add an interesting texture. Dahls always improve from being cooked the day before, allowing the flavours to mature.

250 g packet of mung beans
3 tablespoon oil
1 onion, chopped
2 garlic cloves, sliced thinly
1 teaspoon ground cumin

1 teaspoon turmeric
¼ teaspoon cayenne pepper
salt and freshly ground black pepper
crispy topping onions, to garnish

❶ Cook the beans according to the packet instructions.
❷ Meanwhile, heat the oil and fry the onion, garlic and spices for about 5 minutes.

❸ Drain the beans and stir into the pan over a low heat, until the ingredients are well blended. Season to taste.
❹ Transfer to a serving bowl and sprinkle with the topping onions.

Tomato and Kidney Bean Salad

Preparation time: 10 minutes.
Freezing: not recommended. Serves 4.

The colours and flavours of this salad are redolent of the Mediterranean, so it is ideal for a summer lunch. Serve with some Continental-style bread.

500 g (1 lb) tomatoes
215 g can of red kidney beans, rinsed and
   drained
100 g (3½ oz) canned chick peas, rinsed and
   drained

1 red onion, sliced thinly
3 tablespoons shredded basil leaves
2 tablespoons vinaigrette dressing

❶ Skin the tomatoes. This is easily done by pouring boiling water over them in a bowl, leaving for two minutes, and then draining and peeling off the skin with a sharp knife.
❷ Slice the tomatoes and put in a serving bowl.

❸ Add the beans, chick peas, onion and shredded basil.
❹ Leave in a cool place until ready to serve.
❺ Spoon the dressing over, toss and serve.

Red Lettuce and Onion Salad with Beans

Preparation time: 10 minutes.
Freezing: not recommended. Serves 4.

The range of salad leaves is almost as great as the variety of beans available now. For this dish choose a red lettuce – feuille de chêne, lollo rosso or radicchio. Or simply buy one of the convenient ready-prepared salads from the supermarket. Purple basil makes a striking garnish if you can find it.

1 red onion, sliced thinly in rings
1 red lettuce, washed, dried and separated
220 g can of mixed bean salad
215 g can of red kidney beans, rinsed
    and drained

2 tablespoons olive oil
2 tablespoons tomato juice
juice of ½ lemon
1 tablespoon sliced fresh purple basil (optional)
salt and freshly ground black pepper

❶ Separate the onion rings and put in a bowl with the salad leaves.

❷ Toss in the cans of mixed bean salad and red kidney beans.

❸ Whisk together the oil, tomato juice, lemon juice, basil (if using) and seasoning in a small bowl.

❹ Whisk again just before serving and pour over the salad.

❺ Toss the ingredients in the dressing until evenly coated.

Chinese Salad with Leeks

Preparation time: 15 minutes.
Freezing: not recommended. Serves 4.

Aduki beans are frequently used in Chinese cooking, and here they are the star ingredient in a salad where the flavours blend to give an Eastern flavour.

420 g can of aduki beans, rinsed and drained
50 g (2 oz) bean sprouts, rinsed
227 g can of bamboo shoots, drained
    and sliced
1 small Chinese cabbage, shredded
2 leeks, sliced thinly on the diagonal
1 tablespoon chopped fresh coriander

For the dressing:
2.5 cm (1-inch) piece of fresh root ginger,
    grated
1 tablespoon sesame oil
1 tablespoon light soy sauce
1 tablespoon lime or lemon juice
salt and freshly ground black pepper

❶ Put all the salad ingredients in a bowl and toss together.

❷ Whisk together the dressing ingredients.

❸ Before serving, pour the dressing over the salad and toss together well.

Vegetarian Dishes

The increase in the popularity and variety of beans and pulses available must be in some way due to the growth of vegetarianism. In many cultures where meat is not eaten, beans and pulses are often combined. In some dishes I have mixed together two cuisines, as in the Curried Pasta Bake (page 60) and the Bean Ratatouille (page 62). Gone are the days of the nut cutlet as the only vegetarian alternative!

Chick Peas in Curry Sauce

Preparation time: 10 minutes + 10 minutes cooking.
Freezing: recommended before adding the yogurt.
Serves 4 as a snack or side dish.

This is an Indian version of beans on toast. It could be served as a snack on its own or as a side dish with a curry.

1 tablespoon vegetable oil

1 onion, chopped

420 g can of chick peas, drained

100 g (3½ oz) curry paste, strength according to taste

4 papads or popadoms or 2 naan breads

150 g (5 oz) tub of Greek-style yogurt

salt and freshly ground black pepper

❶ Heat the oil in a pan and cook the onion gently for 5 minutes.

❷ Add the chick peas and curry paste and stir together until blended and piping hot.

❸ Heat through the bread of your choice, according to the packet instructions.

❹ Just before serving, stir the yogurt into the chick peas and heat through without boiling.

❺ Season to taste and spoon onto the breads.

Curried Bean and Mushroom Pie

Preparation time: 5 minutes + 20 minutes cooking.
Freezing: recommended. Serves 4.

Filo pastry is so easy to use, and although the end results look as though you must have spent a lot of time in the kitchen, the opposite is actually true. You could use ordinary baked beans or chilli beans for this recipe.

1 tablespoon sunflower oil

125 g (4 oz) butter

2 onions, chopped coarsely

250 g (8 oz) chestnut mushrooms, sliced

2 × 420 g cans of curried beans

4 sheets of filo pastry

❶ Preheat the oven to Gas Mark 5/190°C/375°F.

❷ Heat the oil and half the butter in a pan and fry the onions and mushrooms for 5 minutes.

❸ Put in a shallow l-litre (1¾-pint) ovenproof dish. Add the beans.

❹ Melt the remaining butter and brush some on one filo sheet. Arrange the sheet on top of the dish, butter-side up, and tuck the sides in or crumple, if necessary.

❺ Repeat with a second sheet.

❻ Cut the remaining two sheets into 1 cm (½-inch) wide ribbons. Arrange on top of the pie.

❼ Brush with the remaining melted butter and bake for 20 minutes, until golden.

Pea Pilaff

Preparation time: 10 minutes + 30 minutes cooking.
Freezing: recommended. Serves 4.

A pilaff is spiced rice to which various ingredients can be added. This particular recipe has the advantage of providing a full complement of proteins.

2 tablespoons vegetable oil

1 onion, chopped

2 garlic cloves, sliced

1 cinnamon stick, broken in 4

8 cloves

12 peppercorns

12 coriander seeds

2 bay leaves

250 g (8 oz) basmati rice

50 g (2 oz) sultanas

750 ml (1¼ pints) water

540 g can of processed peas, rinsed
   and drained

salt and freshly ground black pepper

❶ Heat the oil in a pan and fry the onion and garlic until golden.

❷ Add the spices and bay leaves and fry for 3 minutes.

❸ Stir in the rice and sultanas, and slowly add the water.

❹ Bring to the boil, stirring occasionally, and then reduce to a simmer and cover.

❺ After 15 minutes, add the peas and cook for 5 minutes, or until all the liquid is absorbed. Season to taste before serving.

Curried Pasta Bake

Preparation time: 5 minutes + 20 minutes cooking.
Freezing: recommended. Serves 2–3.

This is a real mix of cuisines – Italian and Indian – but it tastes great and is quick to prepare. Any pasta shapes can be used.

175 g (6 oz) pasta shapes

447 g can of mixed beans in a mild curry
   sauce

50 g (2 oz) butter

6 tablespoons fresh breadcrumbs

salt and freshly ground black pepper

❶ Cook the pasta according to the packet instructions. Drain.

❷ Return the pasta to the pan and add the beans.

❸ Stir together until piping hot, and season to taste.

❹ Pour into an ovenproof serving dish. Preheat the grill.

❺ Melt the butter and stir in the breadcrumbs.

❻ Spoon over the dish and grill until crisp and golden on top.

Bean Ratatouille

Preparation time: 30 minutes + 30 minutes cooking.
Freezing: recommended. Serves 4.

Black beans provide a good visual contrast with the red and green vegetables. Although the cooking time is fairly long, you need pay little attention to it as it simmers. I think that the flavour of ratatouille improves greatly if it is made the day before. This will require a little planning as the beans will need soaking the day before. You could, of course, freeze some cooked black beans and use them as and when required.

2 tablespoons olive oil

1 onion, chopped coarsely

2 garlic cloves, sliced

2 teaspoons mixed dried herbs

1 aubergine, sliced lengthways

1 each red and green pepper, de-seeded and
    chopped

2 courgettes, sliced

250 g (8 oz) black beans, soaked, cooked and
    drained according to packet instructions

230 g can of chopped tomatoes

salt and freshly ground black pepper

❶ Heat the oil in a large pan or flameproof casserole.

❷ Cook the onion, garlic and herbs for 5 minutes, until softened but not browned.

❸ Add the aubergine, cover and cook for 5 minutes.

❹ Add the peppers, cover again and cook for 10 minutes.

❺ Add the courgettes, cover again and cook for 10 minutes more.

❻ Add the prepared beans and canned tomatoes and simmer for 30 minutes.

❼ Season to taste before serving.

Courgette and Soya Bean Tian

Preparation time: 5 minutes + 30 minutes cooking.
Freezing: recommended. Serves 4.

A tian is a Provençale earthenware casserole. The gratin-type dish cooked in it has also become known as a tian. Green vegetables such as spinach, courgettes and marrows are the star ingredients but they can be stretched with beans or rice. This dish can also be served cold.

2 tablespoons olive oil

1 onion, sliced

2 garlic cloves, sliced

500 g (1 lb) courgettes, sliced

1 tablespoon chopped fresh basil

420 g can of soya beans, drained

125 g (4 oz) Gruyère cheese, grated

125 g (4 oz) natural breadcrumbs

salt and freshly ground black pepper

❶ Preheat the oven to Gas Mark 6/200°C/400°F.

❷ Heat the oil in a pan and fry the onion, garlic and courgettes until the vegetables have softened – about 10–15 minutes.

❸ Stir in the basil and the soya beans.

❹ Season to taste and transfer to an ovenproof dish.

❺ Mix together the cheese and breadcrumbs and sprinkle over the top.

❻ Bake for 20 minutes.

Aduki and Savoury Stir-fry

Preparation time: 10 minutes + 10 minutes cooking.
Freezing: not recommended.
Serves 3 as a main dish or 4–5 as a side dish.

This stir-fry could be made with other types of cabbage or using canned beans. I think that the dark red aduki beans go well with the brilliant green colour and bubbly texture of Savoy cabbage.

500 g (1 lb) Savoy cabbage

1 tablespoon vegetable oil

2 garlic cloves, sliced

2.5 cm (1-inch) piece of fresh root ginger, peeled and chopped

420 g can of aduki beans, rinsed and drained

1 tablespoon light soy sauce

1 tablespoon sesame oil

❶ Remove any damaged outer leaves from the cabbage. Quarter and remove the core, and cut in 5 mm (¼-inch) shreds. Rinse and drain.

❷ Heat the oil in a wok and fry the garlic and ginger.

❸ Add the shredded cabbage to the wok and stir-fry for 5 minutes.

❹ Add the beans and stir-fry until heated through.

❺ Spoon the soy sauce and sesame oil over and toss together. Serve immediately.

Tricolour Purée

Preparation time: 15 minutes + 30 minutes cooking.
Freezing: recommended. Serves 4.

This recipe looks so pretty arranged in a round dish like spokes of a wheel, or in stripes in an oblong dish. The golden rule when making potato purée is to not use a food processor which will break down the starches and make it gluey. Most root vegetables can be treated in the same way as the carrots in this recipe. Overlap the cooking of the three vegetables so that they are ready at the same time. Serve with toast or fried bread to add a contrasting crunchy texture.

500 g (1 lb) potatoes, peeled and chopped
2 garlic cloves, skinned
75 g (3 oz) butter
300 g (10 oz) Greek-style yogurt
500 g (1 lb) carrots, peeled and chopped

1 teaspoon ground cumin
500 g packet of frozen peas
1 tablespoon chopped fresh parsley
salt and freshly ground black pepper

❶ Cook the potatoes in lightly salted boiling water with the garlic cloves for 20 minutes. Drain and mash by hand or using an electric food mixer, adding 25 g (1 oz) butter and 100 g (3½ oz) of yogurt. Season to taste and keep warm.

❷ Meanwhile, cook the carrots in lightly salted boiling water for 15 minutes. Drain and mash with 25 g (1 oz) butter, 100 g (3½ oz) yogurt and the ground cumin. Keep warm.

❸ Meanwhile, cook the peas according to the packet instructions. Drain and mash with the remaining butter and yogurt. Beat the parsley in and season to taste.

❹ Arrange the three purées in a warm serving dish.

Baked Potatoes with Bean Topping

Preparation time: 5 minutes + 2 minutes cooking.
Freezing: recommended. Serves 2.

Cans of mixed beans in savoury sauces add instant flavour to potatoes.

2 baking potatoes
50 g (2 oz) butter
447 g can of mixed beans in chilli sauce

1 garlic clove, crushed
1 tablespoon chopped fresh coriander
salt and freshly ground black pepper

❶ Cut a cross in the top of each potato. Bake in a microwave: for a 650W/B oven cook for 9–10 minutes on HIGH; for a 750W/D oven cook for 8–9 minutes on HIGH. Or cook for 1 hour in a preheated oven at Gas Mark 7/220°C/425°F.
❷ When baked, lightly squeeze to soften the flesh, and then cut open at the cross and put 25 g (1 oz) butter in each potato.
❸ Meanwhile heat the beans through with the crushed garlic. Stir in the coriander and season to taste.
❹ Spoon on the top of the baked potatoes.

Vegetable and Hazelnut Rissoles

Preparation time: 10 minutes + 10 minutes cooking.
Freezing: recommended. Makes 8 rissoles.

Puréed peas or lentils provide just the right texture for shaping into rissoles, and their flavour is enhanced by other vegetables.

540 g can of peas or 2 × 420 g cans
  of green lentils
1 onion, chopped finely or grated
2 carrots, peeled and grated
1 tablespoon garlic purée

2 teaspoons mixed herbs
1 egg, beaten
50 g packet of chopped hazelnuts
oil, for frying
salt and freshly ground black pepper

❶ Drain the peas or lentils and whizz them in a blender or liquidiser. Transfer the purée to a bowl.
❷ Stir in the onion, carrots, garlic and herbs. Add enough beaten egg to bind the mixture and season to taste.
❸ Divide into eight and, using wetted hands, shape into round flat patties.
❹ Press the hazelnuts into the patties.
❺ Heat the oil in a frying-pan and fry the rissoles gently for 6 minutes on each side.

Bean-stuffed Acorn Squash

Preparation time: 10 minutes + 45 minutes cooking.
Freezing: recommended. Serves 4.

Squashes are a versatile group of vegetables, but the nearest many of us get to them is carving a face out of a pumpkin at Hallowe'en, or cooking a stuffed marrow in the autumn. Treat this acorn squash in the same way as you would a marrow. By using beans in the stuffing, it becomes a main-course vegetarian dish.

1 acorn squash
1 tablespoon vegetable oil
1 onion, chopped
1 garlic clove, crushed
230 g can of chopped tomatoes

1 tablespoon tomato purée
420 g can of black-eyed beans, rinsed
  and drained
1 tablespoon chopped fresh parsley
salt and freshly ground black pepper

❶ Preheat the oven to Gas Mark 6/200°C/400°F.

❷ Cut a lid from the squash and discard the seeds from the inside of the squash and the lid.

❸ Heat the oil in a pan and gently fry the onion and garlic.

❹ Add the tomatoes and purée, and cook for 5 minutes.

❺ Stir in the beans and parsley, and season to taste.

❻ Stand the squash on a baking sheet or ovenproof dish and spoon the stuffing inside. Replace the lid and cover the stalk with foil so that it does not burn.

❼ Bake in the middle of the oven for about 35 minutes, or until the squash is tender when tested with a skewer or sharp knife.

Party Dishes

When entertaining large numbers of people, economy has to be one of the rules. The use of beans, especially dried beans, as a base for large-scale dishes certainly does help to cut down costs. The dried beans can be pre-cooked and frozen for the sake of convenience (see page 4).

You may need to borrow large pans and dishes for party cooking. I find preserving pans and roasting tins useful for cooking for large numbers. To keep the clearing up as quick and easy as the cooking, use disposable plates and cutlery.

Baked Bean Pasties

Preparation time: 15 minutes + 30 minutes cooking.
Freezing: recommended. Serves 6.

These pasties can be put in packed lunches or picnic boxes. I have added bacon and leeks for extra flavour, but the bacon could be omitted to make the pasties suitable for vegetarians.

420 g can of baked beans
125 g (4 oz) bacon cubes or lean bacon
  rashers, chopped coarsely
1 leek, sliced thinly
1 tablespoon brown sauce

250 g packet of chilled shortcrust pastry
a little flour, for rolling out
1 egg, beaten
salt and freshly ground black pepper

❶ Preheat the oven to Gas Mark 6/200°C/400°F.

❷ Mix together the beans, bacon, leek and brown sauce in a bowl, and season to taste.

❸ Roll the pastry out on a floured surface and cut out six 15 cm (6-inch) circles.

❹ Divide the filling between the circles, spooning it into the centres.

❺ Wet the pastry edges and fold.

❻ Crimp the edges and transfer to a baking sheet.

❼ Brush with beaten egg and bake for 20–30 minutes, until golden brown. Cover with kitchen foil if they brown too quickly.

Baked Bean Moussaka

Preparation time: 20 minutes + 1 hour cooking.
Freezing: recommended without the cheese topping.
Serves 12.

This Greek-inspired dish is relatively easy and quick for a party dish.
Take all the short-cuts you want by using ready-prepared ingredients
– frozen sliced onions, grated cheese, etc.

1 large aubergine, sliced thinly

2 tablespoons salt

3 tablespoons vegetable oil

3 onions, sliced

2 garlic cloves, sliced

840 g can of baked beans

400 g can of chopped tomatoes

1 tablespoon mixed herbs

2 tablespoons olive oil

450 g (15 oz) Greek-style yogurt

2 eggs, beaten

250 g (8 oz) Cheddar cheese, grated

salt and freshly ground black pepper

❶ Sprinkle the aubergine slices with the salt and leave in a colander or sieve for 30 minutes.

❷ Meanwhile, preheat the oven to Gas Mark 4/180°C/350°F.

❸ Heat the vegetable oil in a pan and fry the onions and garlic gently for 5 minutes.

❹ Add the baked beans, tomatoes and herbs and mix well. Bring to the boil, stirring constantly. Season well.

❺ Pour into a large shallow ovenproof dish (a roasting tin is a good alternative).

❻ Rinse the aubergines and pat dry. Arrange over the bean and tomato filling.

❼ Sprinkle the olive oil over the aubergines and season again.

❽ Mix together the yogurt and eggs. Season and pour over the dish, spreading it out evenly.

❾ Cover with the grated cheese and bake in the centre of the oven for 1 hour, or until the top is golden brown.

Chilli con Carne

Preparation time: 20 minutes + 45 minutes cooking.
Freezing: recommended. Serves 12.

This is the archetypal party dish which can be made as hot as you like with the addition of extra chilli powder, chilli sauce or fresh chopped chillies. Serve with boiled rice or crusty bread.

2 tablespoons vegetable oil

2 onions, chopped

4 garlic cloves, sliced

1–2 teaspoons chilli powder

1 kg (2 lb) minced beef or turkey

1 tablespoon mixed dried herbs

400 g can of chopped tomatoes

170 g can of tomato purée

2 × 500 g packets of red kidney beans, soaked, cooked and drained according to packet instructions

salt and freshly ground black pepper

❶ Heat the oil in a large pan and fry the onions, garlic and chilli powder gently for 5 minutes.

❷ Add the minced meat and herbs and cook, stirring frequently, until browned.

❸ Stir in the tomatoes and purée and the cooked beans. Season to taste.

❹ Bring to the boil, and then cover and simmer for 30 minutes.

Vegetable Curry

Preparation time: 20 minutes + 30 minutes cooking.
Freezing: recommended. Serves 12.

This is an ideal party dish which is suitable for vegetarians. All types of vegetables can be added to the basic recipe. Some of the frozen prepared vegetable packets are ideal, e.g. mixed peppers or casserole vegetables. Serve with the usual curry accompaniments – rice, chutneys and Indian bread.

3 tablespoons vegetable oil

3 onions, chopped

6 garlic cloves, sliced

200 g jar of curry paste

500 g packet of country bean mixture, soaked and cooked according to the packet instructions

400 g can of chopped tomatoes

1 kg (2 lb) mixed prepared vegetables (see recipe introduction)

600 ml (1 pint) water or vegetable stock

salt and freshly ground black pepper

❶ Heat the oil in a large pan and fry the onions and garlic until golden brown. Stir in the curry paste.

❷ Add the prepared beans, tomatoes, vegetables and water or stock.

❸ Season lightly and bring to the boil.

❹ Reduce to a simmer and cook for 30 minutes, or until the vegetables are cooked through.

❺ Season to taste before serving.

Quick Cassoulet

Preparation time: 10 minutes + 20 minutes cooking.
Freezing: not recommended. Serves 12.

If you are making this dish for really large numbers, you'll certainly save money by using dried beans and raw meats, and cooking the cassoulet in a traditional slow manner. However, this version is very tasty and takes under 30 minutes from start to finish.

4 tablespoons vegetable oil

4 onions, chopped coarsely

2 × 227 g packets of garlic smoked pork
    sausage, sliced

600 ml (1 pint) chicken stock

400 g can of chopped tomatoes

1 tablespoon Dijon mustard

2 tablespoons tomato purée

2 tablespoons garlic purée

2 × 420 g cans of cannellini beans, drained

420 g can of pinto beans, drained

420 g can of baked beans

24 ready-to-eat roast chicken portions

4 bay leaves

salt and freshly ground black pepper

❶ Heat the oil in a large pan or flameproof casserole and fry the onions and sausage for 5 minutes.

❷ Add the stock, tomatoes, mustard, and tomato and garlic purées, and stir together.

❸ Add the remaining ingredients with a little seasoning.

❹ Bring to the boil and then cover and simmer for 10 minutes.

❺ Check the seasoning before serving.